CAMPAIGN IN
WESTERN VIRGINIA

ARMY OF THE POTOMAC

REPORT OF MAJ.-GEN.
GEORGE B. MCCLELLAN,
AUG. 4, 1863.

WITH AN ACCOUNT OF THE

CAMPAIGN IN WESTERN VIRGINIA

NEW YORK:
SHELDON AND COMPANY,
335 BROADWAY, CORNER OF WORTH STREET.
1864.

MARK S. PHILLIPS PUBLISHING
PROCTORVILLE, OHIO

Entered according to Act of Congress, in the year 1864, by
SHELDON & COMPANY.

In the Clerk's Office of the District Court of the United States for
the Southern District of New York.

250 Copies Printed

C. A. Alvord, Printer.

©2008. All rights reserved.

No part of this book may be reproduced or transmitted
in any form, by any means
(electronic, photocopying, recording, or otherwise)
without the prior written permission
of the publisher.

Library of Congress Catalog Card Number: 2007941375
ISBN-13: 978-0-9667246-3-9

Cover image/frontispiece courtesy the
United States Library of Congress

First Edition

Printed in the United States of America

Mark S. Phillips Publishing
P.O. Box 1208
Proctorville, OH 45669-1208

www.marksphillips.com

TABLE OF CONTENTS

Campaign in Western Virginia 1

Selected Correspondence 46

Afterword by Tim McKinney 63

Index 72

ON TO VICTORY.

GEN. McCLELAN'S WAR SONG!

Forward! Men and meet the foe—
 You strike for your chosen land!
Let the tramp, tramp of your marching feet,
 Be the guide to your steady hand.
Remember how your sires have fought—
 Remember your wrongs of old—
And fight for right and justice
 Till your hearts' red blood run cold.

Ye came from many a far-off clime,
 And speak in many a tongue,
But Freedom's song will reach the heart
 In whatever language sung.
Then wake your voices; let them ring,
 From mountain-side to sea,
In one glad chorus—"GOD PROTECT
 OUR HOME AND LIBERTY!"

Remember, men, what cause ye bear—
 Our nation in one fold—
And cry it forth till the woods resound,
 And the mountain-echoes roll;
And let it be your proudest boast,
 Your dearest-honored fame,
To have won your laurels in the light
 Of that great country's name.

Your lov'd States shall glow with pride,
 From Vermont's wide plains
To Carolina's blood-crimsoned fields—
 Your deeds shall cleanse their stains;
And every man who falls shall leave,
 Above the grassy sod,
The name of one who fought and died
 For Freedom and his God.

CAMPAIGN IN WESTERN VIRGINIA

The attack upon Fort Sumter, on the 12th April, 1861, took the Northern people by surprise, and found them entirely unprepared to carry on a serious contest. Our people were born and educated amidst the blessings of peace and material prosperity; they were in the habit of yielding obedience to the laws of the country and the will of the majority as expressed in the elections, and had become accustomed to see great political excitement and animosity calmly subside through the deference of the minority to the decision of the majority. Thus, to the last moment, it was difficult to realize that a great civil war was imminent; and men clung fondly to the hope that the good sense of both sections would in the eleventh hour find some honorable solution of the difficulty, as had so often been the case before.

It is probable that neither section fully realized the power and violence of the passions evoked, and that each flattered itself with the delusive hope that the other would yield something, rather than risk the inevitable and terrible consequences of an appeal to arms. Each underrated the strength, resources, and courage of the other. These mutual misunderstandings, ably used by a comparatively small number of ambitious and unscrupulous men, were at their height when the insult offered the national flag in the harbor of Charleston aroused both parties to something like a true sense of their condition. The South were warned that they were irrevocably committed to make good their threats, and to establish by force their vaunted right of secession. It was brought clearly to the minds of the Northern men that it was now too late to inquire what were the original causes of the contest, and that it only remained for them to avenge the insult to the flag, and to sustain the government in supporting the inviolability of the Constitution, maintaining the unity of the nation, and enforcing its laws. There can be no question that these were the true issues which called forth that wonderful enthusiasm manifested by our people in 1861. When the President, on the 19th of April, 1861, issued his call for seventy-five thousand volunteers to suppress the rebellion, the difficulty was to restrain the ardor of the nation, and to limit the number of volunteers to something like that called for. The struggle then was as to who should be so fortunate as to be received, not as to who should avoid the call.

The governors of States were besieged by eager crowds, anxious to be permitted to fight for their country; and they, in turn, importuned the authorities in Washington for permission to increase their quotas—a permission usually very difficult to obtain—for the men were still few who foresaw the magnitude and duration of the struggle in which we had embarked.

While there was no difficulty in procuring men, it was no easy task to arm, equip, and organize them, especially in the Western States.

The scanty supplies of war material at the disposal

of the general government were mainly in the East, with the exception of the arms at the St. Louis arsenal, which were not much more than sufficient to meet the demands in Missouri. There was no United States arsenal in the States of Ohio, Indiana, Illinois, or Kentucky. The West at that time possessed no establishment capable of manufacturing arms on a large scale, and few for the preparation of clothing and equipments. In proportion to the population, there was much less military information in the West than in the East.

It was under these circumstances that, on the 23d of April, 1861, I was appointed by Governor Dennison Major-General of the Ohio contingent, under the three months' call, and at once undertook the task of rendering available for the field the mass of unorganized and unarmed men who were collecting upon the call of the President. From Ohio thirteen regiments of infantry were demanded; in a few weeks the same number of three-years regiments was called for, and by the middle of July the number was increased to twenty-two. No cavalry or artillery were embraced in the original call.

On the 23rd of April, there were in the State of Ohio one thousand eight hundred and eighty small arms, mostly altered flint-locks; thirty-one field-guns, many of which were unfit for service, and few provided with the indispensable equipments; one hundred and twenty tents; not a regiment yet mustered into the United States service. Such were the preparations of a State which has since sent vast armies into the field. Indiana and Illinois were not in a more favorable condition.

All mail communications with Washington were at that time interrupted, in consequence of the occurrences at Baltimore, and were for a long period difficult and uncertain. The attention of the authorities was fully occupied in arranging for the immediate defence of the capital, and—the supplies being limited in amount—but little could be done for the Western States, which were for some weeks compelled to rely on their own resources. Neither the people nor the governors failed in the emergency, but both manfully met the crisis. It was then that the strength and value of the State governments were made fully manifest, for to them was the safety of the West due in that hour of trial.

I have good reason to know that all the loyal governors of the Western States did their full duty in the emergency; but being in more direct personal communication with Governor Dennison of Ohio, during the most critical portion of this period, I desire to bear testimony to the high qualities he then displayed. He manifested a degree of energy, ability, untiring devotion, and disinterested patriotism which was creditable in the extreme.

As has already been said, the Western States were totally unprepared for the impending struggle. It may be asserted with almost literal truth, that neither arms, ammunition, nor equipments existed there; we had nothing but the men—all else was to be created. Another great difficulty arose from absence of government funds; the subsistence department soon supplied its agents with money, but none was received from the quarter-master's department until after the 20th of May, and then for some time in insufficient amounts.

The governors of the States now exerted themselves to the utmost; they were energetically supported by the Legislatures, who authorized them to use the funds and pledge the credit of their States for the purchase of arms, ammunition, clothing, etc. Without this action on their part, the greater portion of the summer would have passed without the organization of troops in the West.

On the 3d of May, the States of Ohio, Indiana, and Illinois were formed into the Department of the Ohio, which the General-in-chief placed under my command. Immediately upon receiving the order, I placed myself in communication with the governors of these three States, and nothing in our power was left undone to push forward military preparations. The governor of Ohio, fully alive to the magnitude of the occasion, and the insufficiency of the number of troops called for, had, by the close of April, obtained the authority of the Legislature to form nine regiments of three-months troops for the service of the State, in addition to those called for by the United States. He placed these additional regiments under my command. It was only after repeated efforts and refusals that a very small number of regular officers were obtained to take charge of the administrative branches of the service, and the task of organization slowly proceeded.

Supplies did not come in rapidly, and great difficulty was experienced in arming and equipping the troops.

On the 21st of May, the total number of small arms in the State of Ohio was twenty-five thousand one hundred and seventy-nine, of which twenty-two thousand and seventy-five were smooth-bores, mostly very inferior specimens of the altered flint-locks. Infantry equipments were still more difficult to obtain.

During the month of May, the political aspect of affairs in Kentucky and Western Virginia was uncertain and threatening. In the latter, a convention had been called to assemble at Wheeling, on the 13th of May, to decide upon the question of separation from the eastern portion of the State, while the election upon the question of ratifying the Richmond ordinance of secession from the United States, was fixed for the 23d of the same month. Excitement ran high, and honest men differed widely as to the policy that should be pursued by the military authorities of the general government.

I received a multitude of letters from a large number of sincere Union men, who entertained widely divergent views as to the measures adequate to the emergency. Many urged, as early as the beginning of May, that troops should immediately be sent into Virginia, to encourage the Union men and prevent the secessionists from gaining a foothold. At least an equal number insisted, with equal force, that the arrival of troops from other States would merely arouse State pride, throw many wavering men into the rebel ranks, and at once kindle the flames of civil war.

In Kentucky, the struggle was much more bitter than in Western Virginia. The State government, the arms, and the military organization, were to a great extent in the hands of men who favored the secession of the State; but so able and determined was the course of the Union leaders, and so marked did the majority of the people soon become in their support, that the secessionist leaders were compelled to content themselves with the avowal of the position of neutrality, while awaiting the results of the elections to be held on the 26th June for Congressmen, and on the 4th August for members of the Legislature.

The policy of the leaders of the Union party was, "To remain in the Union without a revolution, under all the forms of law, and by their own action." The words of Garret Davis were: "We will remain in the Union by voting if we can, by fighting if we must, and if we cannot hold our own, we will call on the general government to aid us."

It was the desire of these true and able men that no extraneous elements of excitement should be introduced in the State until the elections were over; they felt sure of carrying these elections, if left to themselves. I fully coincided with them in their expectations and opinions, and, so far as was in my power, lent them every assistance in carrying out their views, among which wee the organization of Home Guards and the distribution of arms to Union men. In Missouri, hostilities had already broken out, and it was evident that that State was destined to become the seat of serious fighting; nor was it then supposed that our tenure of St. Louis was entirely secure.

Collections of Southern troops at Memphis and Union City threatened Columbus, Ky., and Cairo, and made it necessary to keep a vigilant watch in that direction. It should also be remembered that in the early part of May the national capital was by no means secure, and it was not at that time an improbable contingency that Western regiments might yet be needed to protect or regain Washington. As bearing upon this point, it may be stated, that in a letter addressed to the General-in-chief, on the 21st May, I informed him that from the information in my possession, the indications were that the disposable troops in the regular Confederate service, from Mississippi, Alabama, Arkansas, and Louisiana, had gone to the East *via* Lynchburg; leaving in Tennessee the State militia, who were badly armed, and under no discipline. On the 26th April, when my command was confined to the limits of the State of Ohio, I submitted to the General-in-chief certain suggestions, the substance of which was: That, for the purposes of defence, Cairo should be occupied by two battalions, strongly intrenched, and provided with heavy guns, and a gunboat to control the river; that some eight battalions should be stationed at Sandoval, in Illinois, to observe St. Louis, sustain the garrison of Cairo, and, if necessary, reinforce Cincinnati; that a few companies would observe the lower Wabash; that some four thousand men would be posted at Seymour, in Indiana, to observe Louisville, and be ready to support either Cincinnati or Cairo; that there should be five thousand men at or near Cincinnati, and two battalions at Chillicothe, Ohio. With the troops disposable for active operations, it was proposed to move up the valley of the Great Kanawha upon Richmond; this movement to be made with the greatest promptness, that it might not fail to relieve Washington, or to insure the destruction of the enemy in Eastern Virginia, if aided by a prompt advance on the eastern line of operations. Should Kentucky assume a hostile attitude, it was recommended to cross the Ohio with eighty thousand men, and move straight on Nashville, acting thence in concert with a vigorous offensive on the Eastern line. It was strongly urged that every thing possible should be done to hasten the equipment and armament of the Western troops, as the nation would be entirely deprived of their powerful aid until this should be accomplished.

It was not until the 13th May that the order forming the Department of the Ohio, and assigning me to the command, was received. In the mean time, as much excitement existed at Cincinnati, which city was regarded as a tempting object to the enemy in the uncertain condition of Kentucky, I took steps to concentrate the greater part of the Ohio troops at Camp Dennison, on the Little Miami Railroad, seventeen miles from Cincinnati; a favorable position for instruction, and presenting peculiar facilities for movement in any direction. As soon as the new department was placed under my command, I took steps for the immediate erection of heavy batteries at Cairo. In the letter of May 21st, already referred to, after giving the information obtained in regard to the position of the enemy on the Mississippi River, it was stated that I was convinced of the necessity of having, without a day's delay, a few efficient gunboats to operate from Cairo as a base; that if they were rendered shot-proof, they would enable us at least to annoy seriously the rebel camps on the Mississippi, and interfere with their river communications—their main dependence; that I requested authority to make the necessary expenditures to procure gunboats, and that I regarded them as an indispensable element in any system of operations whether offensive or defensive. In the same letter the necessity for light batteries was strongly set forth.

I now urged to the utmost the organization and equipment of the troops in the three States, and received the most energetic and cordial support from Governors Morton, Yates, and Dennison. While awaiting the development of the policy of the general government, and in accordance with the sound advice of the General-in-chief as to the instruction of the troops, I determined to hold the troops in readiness to move wherever they might be needed, and to push the work of instruction and equipment. I also determined to afford any assistance in my power that might be required by the commanding officer in Missouri, and so informed him; to take no steps of a military nature in Kentucky until after the elections, unless that State were invaded from Tennessee, in which case I clearly informed all concerned that I would at once cross the Ohio and drive out the invaders; and, in regard to Western Virginia, to await the result of the convention of May 13 and the election of May 23, with the purpose of moving before that time, if the operations of the secessionists became such as to require attention.

In the early part of May, I declined moving troops into Western Virginia for the reasons already given, and because I regarded Kentucky as of much greater importance. It was not until the latter part of the month that I became fully satisfied as to the favorable tendency of affairs in that quarter.

It was difficult to obtain accurate information as to

the movements of the secessionists in Western Virginia, and the results proved that it was always necessary to make great allowances for the exaggeration which ever attends ignorance of military affairs, and the alarm consequent upon the shock produced by a novel and abnormal state of things. Early in May, Governor Letcher called out the militia of Western Virginia, under the State laws; Charleston in the Great Kanawha Valley, Parkersburg in Wood County, and Grafton in Taylor County, being the points at which time they were to be assembled. The accounts we received at the time, in regard to the numbers of the militia thus collected, varied much, and great alarm frequently manifested itself on the Ohio frontier, lest it should be invaded. To quiet this not unnatural feeling, a few arms were distributed among the Home Guards, and about the middle of May some regiments of the Ohio State troops were moved to points convenient to the more exposed portions of the frontier. I did not share the apprehensions of an invasion, for I saw no good reason to suspect the existence of the necessary preparations, and did not regard it as probable that the Confederates would at that period consider Western Virginia as a suitable base for offensive operations north and west of the Ohio River. I supposed it to be the object of the Richmond authorities to hold possession of Western Virginia, and to coerce its loyal inhabitants into the secession movement.

Dispatches from General R.E. Lee to Colonel Porterfield, dated May 4th and later, which were captured at a subsequent period, seem to establish the correctness of this view. In the letter of May 4th,

Colonel Porterfield was directed to repair to Grafton, and select a position for the troops called into the service of the State (Virginia), for the protection and defence of that part of the country. He was informed that orders had already been given for the occupation of Wheeling, and was instructed to take possession of Parkersburg and the railway leading thereto. He was ordered to call out the militia in all the counties north of the Great Kanawha Valley, and informed that it was not intended to interfere with the peaceful use of the Baltimore and Ohio Railroad. In a letter dated Richmond, May 24th, General Lee regrets that Colonel Porterfield has been unsuccessful in organizing volunteers; informs him that reinforcements are on the way from Staunton and Harper's Ferry, and hopes that he will spare no pains to preserve the integrity of the State, and to prevent the occupation of the Baltimore and Ohio Railroad by its enemies. In reply to an inquiry of Colonel Porterfield's as to the treatment of traitors, he says that he cannot believe that any citizen of the State will betray its interests, and that he hopes all will unite in supporting the policy she may adopt.

It was not until the 27th May, that the order was given by Governor Letcher for the seizure of the post-offices at Harper's Ferry and Grafton, and the appointment of postmasters in the interest of the State government. Information had already been received that a small camp of secessionist militia was being established in the immediate vicinity of Grafton, when, on the 24th of May, I received from the Secretary of War and the General-in-chief telegrams confirming the fact of the existence of this camp, and inquiring whether its effect upon the Union men of that region could not be counteracted. I replied that it could be done, and that, if it were desired, the whole region could be cleared of the secessionists. To this I received no reply, nor did I receive any subsequent communication as to sending troops into Western Virginia. I, however, proceeded to make the preparations for sending an expedition to Grafton, as well as another to the Kanawha—the convention of the 13th having proved largely in favor of dividing the State, and the election of the 23d having resulted in a decided refusal to ratify the secession ordinance. These preparations were much interfered with, as were all operations for some weeks subsequently, by the fact that, at that time, all the three-months United States regiments from Ohio were in the course of transition to three-years regiments, so that there were no troops available in Ohio, except the nine regiments in State service.

While at Camp Dennison, on the afternoon of the 26th May, I received intelligence that the secessionists were advancing from Grafton towards Wheeling and Parkersburg, for the purpose of destroying the railroad. Regarding this as an act of hostility, which it was my duty to counteract without delay, I at once returned to Cincinnati, and gave, by telegraph, the orders necessary in the case. In a letter subsequently captured, dated Grafton, May 25th, Colonel Porterfield states to Colonel Willey, that it was essential to the safety of this command that the bridges be destroyed as far west on the railroad as possible, and directs the latter to proceed on the next train to carry the destruction into effect without delay. The 1st Regiment (loyal) Virginia Volunteers was in process of organization at Wheeling, under Colonel B.F. Kelly; the men were provided with muskets, but had no cartridge-boxes, equipments, uniform, or camp-equipage. Late in the afternoon, I telegraphed Colonel Kelly to move his regiment, at an early hour on the 27th, along the Baltimore and Ohio Railroad, in the direction of Fairmont. Colonel Kelly was instructed to prevent any further destruction of the bridges, and to cover the repairs of those already injured; he was directed to move with caution, and to use every effort to preserve discipline, to respect the rights and property of the inhabitants, to conciliate the people, and strengthen the Union feeling.

Colonel Irwin, commanding the 16th Ohio State Regiment, was ordered to move from his camp at Bellaire into Virginia, and support the forward movement of the 1st Virginia.

Colonel Stedman, 14th Ohio, with his own regiment and the 18th, and Barnett's State Battery, was ordered to take possession of Parkersburg on the morning of the 27th, and proceed to Grafton, under orders similar to those of Colonel Kelly.

Deeply impressed with the importance of causing the citizens of West Virginia to understand clearly the true purposes of the occupation of their soil, and desirous to infuse a proper feeling among our new troops, I issued the following proclamation to the inhabitants, and address to the troops.

PROCLAMATION.

HEAD-QUARTERS, DEPARTMENT OF THE OHIO.
MAY 25, 1861

To the Union Men of Western Virginia:

VIRGINIANS!—The general government has long enough endured the machinations of a few factious rebels in your midst. Armed traitors have in vain endeavored to deter you from expressing your loyalty at the polls. Having failed in this infamous attempt to deprive you of the exercise of your dearest rights, they now seek to inaugurate a reign of terror, and thus force you to yield to their schemes, and submit to the yoke of traitorous conspiracy, dignified by the name of the Southern Confederacy. They are destroying the property of citizens of your State, and ruining your magnificent railways. The general government has heretofore carefully abstained from sending troops across the Ohio, or even from posting them along its banks, although frequently urged to do so by many of your prominent citizens. It determined to await the result of the late election, desirous that no one might be able to say that the slightest effort had been made from this side to influence the free expression of your opinions, although the many agencies brought to bear upon you by the rebels were well known. You have now shown, under the most adverse circumstances, that the great mass of the people of Western Virginia are true and loyal to that beneficent government under which we and our fathers have lived so long. As soon as the result of the election was known, the traitors commenced their work of destruction. The general government cannot close its ears to the demand you have made for assistance. I have ordered troops to cross the Ohio River. They come as your friends and brothers,—as enemies only to the armed rebels who are preying upon you. Your homes, your families, and your property are safe under our protection. All your rights shall be religiously respected, notwithstanding all that has been said by the traitors, to induce you to believe that our advent among you will be signalized by interference with your slaves. Understand one thing clearly. Not only will we abstain from all such interference, but we will, on the contrary, with an iron hand, crush any attempt at insurrection on their part. Now that we are in your midst, I call upon you to fly to arms, and support the general government. Sever the connection that binds you to traitors; proclaim to the world that the faith and loyalty so long boasted by the Old Dominion, are still preserved in Western Virginia, and that you remain true to the stars and stripes.

> GEO. B. MCCLELLAN,
> *Major-General U.S.A. Comd'g Dep't.*

ADDRESS.

HEAD-QUARTERS, DEPARTMENT OF THE OHIO.
CINCINNATI, MAY 26, 1861.

SOLDIERS!—You are ordered to cross the frontier, and enter upon the soil of Virginia.

Your mission is to restore peace and confidence, to protect the majesty of the law, and to rescue our brethren, from the grasp of armed traitors. You are to act in concert with Virginia troops, and to support their advance. I place under the safeguard of your honor, the persons and property of the Virginians. I know that you will respect their feelings and all their rights.

Preserve the strictest discipline. Remember that each one of you holds in his keeping the honor of Ohio and the Union. If you are called upon to overcome armed opposition, I know that your courage is equal to the task; but remember that your only foes are the armed traitors,—and show mercy even to them when they are in your power, for many of them are misguided. When, under your protection, the loyal men of Western Virginia have been enabled to organize and arm, they can protect themselves, and you can then return to your homes, with the proud satisfaction of having saved a gallant people from destruction.

> GEO. B. MCCLELLAN,
> *Major-General U.S.A. Comd'g.*

I had received no instructions as to the points covered by these documents, nor had I in fact any direct orders to move troops across the Ohio; nor was there now time to refer to Washington for instructions. These addresses were accordingly prepared in great haste, without consultation, and sent by telegraph to Wheeling and Marietta immediately after the dispatch of the orders for the movement of the troops. On the 1st June, I wrote to the President, informing him of the circumstances under which the proclamation was written; that I had endeavored to express what I had reason to suppose his views to be, and requesting to be informed if I had misconceived the intentions of his excellency. As I received no reply to this letter, nor any intimation from any quarter that my policy was disapproved, I assumed that I was right, and acted accordingly.

Early in the afternoon of the 30th, Colonel Kelly, without the loss of a single man, reached Grafton, which the secessionists had abandoned upon his approach; he had repaired the bridges behind him and established his railway communications with Wheeling. Colonel Stedman arrived at Clarksburg somewhat later, and communicated with Colonel Kelly; great delays had occurred on this line also in consequence of the destruction of the bridges. Steps were at once taken to guard the exposed structures on both branches of the railroad, and reinforcements were pushed forward from Ohio and Indiana. The enemy fell back from Grafton upon Philippi, a village some twenty miles distant, in the direction of Beverly. Brigadier-General T.A. Morris, Indiana Volunteers, was ordered to Grafton, with the 6th, 7th, and 9th Indiana Regiments, to assume the immediate command. He reached his destination about the last day of May, and arranged an expedition to disperse or capture the force at Philippi. He directed the movement to be made in two columns: one under Colonel Kelly, consisting of five companies of the 1st Virginia, and detachments of the 15th and 16th Ohio, and 9th Indiana, to march by a country road east of Tygart's Valley River, and thus reach the rear of Philippi; while Colonel Dumont, 7th Indiana, was to proceed by the turnpike from Webster, with a column consisting of the greater part of the 6th and 7th Indiana, and the 14th Ohio, and two sections of Barnett's Battery, and attack in front. It was intended that the two columns should attack at 4 A.M., on the 3d June; but Colonel Kelly's command was delayed somewhat by the heavy rain which fell during the night, and rendered the country road it followed very bad. Just before Colonel Kelly reached their camp, the enemy received intelligence of his approach, and dispersed. They escaped with the loss of fifteen killed, some wounded and prisoners, many arms, and all their baggage. Our loss was confined to the serious wound received by the gallant Colonel Kelly, who had, from the commencement of the movement from Wheeling, displayed great energy and high soldierly qualities. All the regiments engaged in these trying marches deserve great credit for their endurance and anxiety to meet the enemy; none more so than the 1st Virginia, which made this short campaign destitute of all the necessaries of a soldier, save their muskets and the ammunition they carried in their pockets.

The absence of means of transportation and of cavalry rendered it impossible to follow up this success. Had it been otherwise, our troops might have occupied the Cheat Mountain Pass without opposition, and there probably would have been no immediate necessity for the subsequent campaign in that quarter. As it was, it was necessary to content ourselves with the occupation of Philippi and the Cheat River line until subsequent events called me to the field in person. As fast as the Ohio State regiments were equipped, they were pushed into Western Virginia, and General Morris was thus enabled to provide for the security of the railroad in his rear, and of his advanced positions. Every exertion was now made by Captain J.H. Dickerson, the able chief quartermaster of the department, to provide means of transportation; but notwithstanding his utmost efforts, this work proceeded slowly, and there was a most vexatious delay in all the preparations necessary to put the troops in proper condition to take the field. While these measures were being pushed to the utmost, during the early and middle parts of June, intelligence reached me that strong reinforcements had arrived to the enemy at Beverly, from the East; that General Robert S. Garnett had been placed in command, and that he had occupied strong positions at Laurel Hill and Rich Mountain, commanding the two roads leading to Beverly. Reports reached me almost daily to the effect that his force was being rapidly increased, and that he would soon assume the offensive, to regain what they had lost in Western Virginia. Although many of these reports were evidently exaggerated, and the danger did not appear so imminent as some apprehended, I determined to go thither as soon as a sufficient force could be made available, and, by taking the initiative, dispose of Garnett before he was in condition to do much mischief. The aspect of affairs in Missouri and Tennessee was at this time such, that I did not feel at liberty to make use of the Illinois regiments, but left them for service in the quarter named, and assigned the available Ohio and Indiana troops to duty in West Virginia.

Towards the close of June a considerable amount of transportation was ready, and the arrangements for the supply of camp equipage somewhat advanced. As the reports from Grafton were now very alarming, I determined that the proper time had arrived for me to take the field, and on the 20th June left Cincinnati for Parkersburg, where I arrived the next morning. The 21st and part of the 22nd were spent at that place in hurrying on transportation and supplies, and on the afternoon of the 22nd I went to Grafton, leaving General Rosecrans at Parkersburg to push forward the troops and material. On the 23d I wrote to the General-in-chief from Grafton, informing him that five regiments and two detached companies of infantry, one battery, and one company of cavalry had reached the vicinity, and that two more regiments of infantry and a battery were expected next day; that the information received rendered it more than probable that a rebel force of from one thousand five hundred to three thousand, with guns, was intrenched at Romney; that I thought their purpose was to cover the approaches to Winchester against an attack from the west, and suggesting that General Patterson should take care of them. I also stated that it was now certain that the enemy had a force of some kind near Huttonsville, with a strong advanced party intrenched near Laurel Mountain, between Philippi and Beverly, and that their chief object seemed to me to be to furnish and protect guerrilla parties, which were then doing much mischief; also, that the apprehensions which had existed on the part of our people of an attack by this party of the enemy were not well founded; that as soon as my command was well in hand, and my information more full, I proposed moving, with all my available force, from Clarksburg on Buckhannon, thence on Beverly, to turn entirely the detachment at Laurel Hill; the troops at Philippi to advance in time to follow up the retreat of the enemy in their front. That, after occupying Beverly, I would move on Huttonsville, and drive the enemy into the mountains, whither I did not purpose to follow them unless certain of success. Finally, that after having driven out the mass of their troops, and having occupied the pass by which they might return, I proposed to move small columns through the country, to reassure the Union men and break up all scattered armed parties; and that, as soon as practicable, I intended to clear out the valley of the Kanawha.

This letter contained the plan of campaign which was eventually carried into effect; and it must be observed that its object was simply to drive the enemy out of Western Virginia, and hold it for the general government.

The movement upon which I was now entering was

not in consequence of any specific orders I received from Washington, nor was it a part of any general system of operations. My department was invaded by the enemy, and I proceeded forthwith to drive them out. The idea, very generally entertained, that my operations were intended to aid General Patterson, to threaten Winchester, or menace Richmond, was an erroneous one. I was never informed of the intended plan of campaign in the East, and my suggestion as to movements without the bounds of my department towards the East had not been entertained. I regarded the movement into Western Virginia as a mere interlude, which served to accustom the troops to marches, hardships, and combats, and I intended to return to Cincinnati when it was over, in order to resume the preparations for the more important movements upon East Tennessee, which would, I hoped, soon be undertaken.

While at Grafton, the following addresses to the inhabitants of West Virginia and to the troops were issued, as called for by circumstances at the time:

HEAD-QUARTERS, DEPARTMENT OF THE OHIO, GRAFTON, VA., JUNE 23, 1861

To the Inhabitants of Western Virginia:
The army of this department, headed by Virginia troops, is rapidly occupying all Western Virginia. This is done in cooperation with, and

in support of, such civil authorities of the State as are faithful to the constitution and laws of the United States. The proclamation issued by me, under date of May 26, 1861, will be strictly maintained. Your houses, families, property, and all your rights will be religiously respected; we are enemies to none but armed rebels, and those voluntarily giving them aid. All officers of this army will be held responsible for the most prompt and vigorous action in repressing disorder, and punishing aggression by those under their command.

To my great regret, I find that enemies of the United States continue to carry on a system of hostilities prohibited by the laws of war among belligerent nations, and of course far more wicked and intolerable when directed against loyal citizens engaged in the defence of the common government of all. Individuals and marauding parties are pursuing a guerrilla warfare—firing upon sentinels and pickets, burning bridges, insulting, injuring, and even killing citizens, because of their Union sentiments, and committing many kindred acts.

I do now therefore make proclamation, and warn all persons, that individuals or parties engaged in this species of warfare—irregular in every view which can be taken of it—thus attacking sentinels, pickets, or other soldiers, destroying public or private property, or committing injuries against any of the inhabitants because of union sentiments or conduct, will be dealt with, in their persons and property, according to severest rules of military law.

All persons giving information or aid to the public enemies, will be arrested and kept in close custody; and all persons found bearing arms, unless of known loyalty, will be arrested and held for examination.

Geo. B. McClellan,
Major-General U.S.A. Comd'g

Head-Quarters, Department of the Ohio,
Grafton, Va., June 25, 1861

To the Soldiers of the Army of the West:
You are here to support the government of your country and to protect the lives and liberties of your brethren, threatened by a rebellious and traitorous foe. No higher and nobler duty could devolve upon you, and I expect you to bring to its performance the highest and noblest qualities of soldiers— discipline, courage, and mercy. I call upon the officers of every grade to enforce the strictest discipline, and I know that those of all grades, privates and officers, will display in battle cool heroic courage, and will know how to show mercy to a disarmed enemy.

Bear in mind that you are in the country of friends, not of enemies; that you are here to protect, not to destroy. Take nothing, destroy nothing, unless you are ordered to do so by your general officers. Remember that I have pledged my word to the people of Western Virginia, that their rights in person and property shall be respected. I ask every one of you to make good this promise in its broadest sense. We come here to save, not to upturn. I do not appeal to the fear of punishment, but to your appreciation of the sacredness of the cause in which we are engaged. Carry with you into battle the conviction that you are right, and that God is on your side.

Your enemies have violated every moral law—neither God nor man can sustain them. They have without cause rebelled against a mild and paternal government; they have seized upon public and private property; they have outraged the persons of Northern men merely because they came from the North, and of Southern Union men merely because they loved the Union; they have placed themselves beneath contempt, unless they can retrieve some honor on the field of battle. You will pursue a different course. You will be honest, brave, and merciful; you will respect the right of private opinion; you will punish no man for opinion's sake. Show to the world that you differ from our enemies in the points of honor, honesty, and respect for private opinion, and that we inaugurate no reign of terror where we go.

Soldiers! I have heard that there was danger here. I have come to place myself at your head and to share it with you. I fear now but one thing—that you will not find foemen worthy of your steel. I know that I can rely upon you.

Geo. B. McClellan,
Major-General Comd'g.

It was not until the last of June that the necessary arrangements for an advance were completed; these preparations were much retarded by the fact that while in West Virginia I had no experienced quartermaster with me until the day before I left Grafton for Buckhannon.

It may be well to state here, that the greatest difficulty had been experienced at first from the almost entire want of instructed officers for the various staff departments. Much time and expense would have been saved had we been better provided in this respect at an earlier day.

Before moving from Grafton, the troops in the field were assigned as follows:

Philippi. Brigadier-General Morris with the 6th, 7th, and 9th Indiana, 14th Ohio, three companies of 15th Ohio, four companies of 16th Ohio, four companies of 1st Virginia, and Colonel Barnett's Ohio Battery; the 6th Ohio was subsequently assigned to this command.

Grafton, etc. Brigadier-General Hill, Ohio Militia, in charge of the defence of the railroad and Cheat River, with the 15th, 16th, 18th, 20th, and 22d Ohio State troops, and Captain Dahn's Virginia Battery; other Ohio troops were subsequently added to this command.

Active Column under my own Command. First Brigade, Brigadier-General Rosecrans, 8th and 10th Indiana, 17th and 19th Ohio; the 17th Ohio was subsequently replaced by the 13th Indiana. Second Brigade, Brigadier-General Schleich, with 3d, 4th, 7th, and 10th Ohio; the 7th and 10th were both detached, and did not rejoin the main column during the continuance of active operations.

Attached to Head-Quarters. Captain Barker's and Burdsall's companies of cavalry, Captain Howe's and Loomis's Batteries, 9th Ohio Volunteers, Company I, 4th United States Artillery, company Chicago Rifles, two companies 2d Virginia Infantry.

On the 27th June, General Morris was directed to proceed next morning to Philippi and assume command of the forces at that place. His instructions were to place his command in an attitude to move upon the shortest notice; to keep a watchful eye on the enemy in his front, and to follow closely should they retreat; and if he learned that any portion had retreated by the roads leading to the north and east, to endeavor to cut them off and destroy them.

General Hill, who relieved General Morris at Grafton, received special instructions as to guarding the base of operations, and was directed to pay particular attention to the Cheat River line. The theatre of operations was that portion of Western Virginia contained between the Ohio and Cheat Rivers in one direction, between the Baltimore and Ohio Railroad and the Great Kanawha and Gauley Rivers in the other. The affluents of the Monongahela and the two Kanawhas divide this region into a number of narrow valleys, separated by rough and difficult hills, which become true mountains as they approach the heads of the little Kanawha and the west fork of the Monongahela. The roads practicable for wagons are few, narrow, and difficult. As cultivation is generally confined to the valleys, and the mountain sides are obstructed by rocks and a dense growth of timber and underbrush, it is difficult even for skirmishers to move across the country, and it is not possible for troops and trains to march elsewhere than on the narrow roads. Positions suitable for handling artillery are rare, and cavalry is useful in that district only to convey intelligence. The resources of the country are inconsiderable. There are few regions more difficult for the operations of large bodies of troops. The only practicable wagons roads leading across the mountains into this region, between Lewisburg and Moorefield, unite at Huttonsville, near the head of Tygart's Valley River; from this point northward, there is no practicable wagon road across the mountains until the road leading from Leedsville *via* St. George to West Union and Moorefield is reached. The main turnpike, from Staunton to Wheeling, passes through Huttonsville and Beverly down the Tygart's Valley; this road was held and intrenched by General Garnett at Laurel Hill, some fifteen miles north of Beverly. At the latter place a good road branches off westward to Buckhannon; this road was held and intrenched by Colonel Pegram at Rich Mountain, some five miles west of Beverly. This last road again forks at Buckhannon, one branch leading to Weston, the other to Clarksburg. About twelve miles from the latter place, near a bridge over Elk Creek, a cross-road comes in from Philippi. Premising that the mountains separating the valleys are everywhere impassable for artillery, except by the roads mentioned, it will be easy to understand the movements of the campaign, which were exceedingly simple. The direct and natural retreat of Garnett and Pegram was *via* Huttonsville on Staunton; if cut off from that, their only chance of escape was *via* Leedsville and St. George. Upon these data I arranged the plan of campaign sketched in the letter of June 23, already referred to. On the 26th June, three regiments of Rosecrans's brigade and Loomis's battery were advanced from Clarksburg, twelve miles towards Buckhannon, to Elk Bridge, where the cross-road branches off to Philippi; and on the same day the 9th Ohio was moved from Webster to Philippi, ready at the proper time to join Rosecrans by the cross-road above referred to. The object of these dispositions was to gain more room for movements, to cover the Elk Bridge, and to deceive the enemy as to our real intentions, by drawing their attention to Philippi. General Schleich's brigade followed to Elk Bridge on the 28th. General Rosecrans, with the three regiments of his own brigade, the 9th Ohio, and Loomis's battery, occupied Buckhannon on the 30th. At four A.M., of the same day, Colonel Tyler, of the 7th Ohio, occupied Weston after a night march of twenty-eight miles from Clarksburg, placed the State officers in possession of the Branch Bank at that place, and put a stop to guerrilla operations in that quarter. As Colonel Tyler was thus but one march from Buckhannon, he was in position to support the main column if necessary. He covered our base of operations, and it was hoped that this apparently divergent movement would tend still more to confuse the enemy as to my real designs. General Schleich reached Buckhannon on the 2d July. I had not intended to occupy Buckhannon, nor to advance beyond Elk Bridge, until prepared to pass through Buckhannon to Beverly without halting; but the difficulty of finding proper camping-grounds carried some of the troops beyond Elk Bridge on the 28th, upon learning which I determined to occupy Buckhannon, in order to prevent the enemy from drawing supplies or reinforcements from that region. Having completed my preparations as far as possible, I left Clarksburg on the 1st July, and reached Buckhannon on the 2d. Further delay was incurred here in consequence of the great deficiency in transportation; it being necessary to send back the trains to bring up supplies before we could proceed further. While waiting here, and previously at Clarksburg, several expeditions were sent out from Parkersburg, Weston, etc., to protect loyal citizens, cover the approaches to the railroads, break up guerrilla parties, etc. On the 3d, instructions were sent to General Hill, informing him that, if the enemy at Laurel Hill permitted us to gain their rear at Beverly, their only chance of escape would be by St. George, or by forcing the passage of the Cheat River near Rowlesburg, and directing him to hold his troops in readiness to act should the case occur.

About this time it became certain that Generals Wise and Floyd had reached the Kanawha Valley with considerable reinforcements. I therefore instructed

General J.D. Cox, Ohio Volunteers, to proceed to that region with the 1st and 2d Kentucky, the 11th, 12th, and 21st Ohio, which last regiment had been for some weeks at Gallipolis in observation. On the 10th July General Cox occupied Point Pleasant; on the 11th, Guyandotte. The instructions, sent on the 2d July, directed him to remain on the defensive near the mouth of Ten Mile Creek, and to hold the enemy near Charleston; it being my hope to cut them off after we gained the Cheat Mountain Pass. He was instructed to keep out parties to break up the guerrilla bands and protect Union men. On the 6th, General Cox was placed in command of the District of Kanawha, comprising the country between the two streams of that name. He received instructions for occupying Ripley, Guyandotte, and Barboursville, and was informed of the steps already taken to occupy certain important county towns. He was now also instructed to endeavor to gain possession of Charleston, to drive the enemy beyond the Gauley Bridge, and to open communication with the main force under my command.

On the 6th July, instructions were sent to General Morris, directing him to advance next morning to a position near Elliot's farm, within one and a half miles of the enemy, at Laurel Hill. He was instructed to accomplish this movement at all hazards, and from his new position to push out strong infantry reconnaissances to ascertain the exact position, condition, and movements of the enemy, as well as to give them the impression that the main attack was to be made by him. He was directed to watch them closely day and night, to use all efforts to retain the enemy at

Laurel Hill, the object being to cut off their retreat with the main column at Beverly; he was ordered to hold every thing ready to pursue should they retreat, and to follow them closely in that event.

Finally, he was informed of the intended movements of the main column. On the 8th July, General Morris was again enjoined to watch the enemy closely, and to follow them up should they attempt to retreat.

On the 7th July, the advanced guard, consisting of the 4th and 9th Ohio, Loomis's Battery, and the company of Ohio cavalry, all under Colonel R.L. McCook, of the 9th Ohio, moved from Buckhannon to the Middle Fork Bridge; they seized this important bridge after a slight skirmish, and halted there during the 8th to await supplies. Rosecrans's brigade was ordered to move to the same point at 4 a.m., on the 8th; Schleich's, at a later hour; head-quarters between the two brigades.

The 10th Ohio had just arrived, and was ordered to move with its brigade; but at the moment when head-quarters were starting, intelligence arrived of a serious attack by the enemy upon a detachment at Glenville, and it became necessary to detach that regiment to support the troops in that region.

On the afternoon of the 9th, the main column reached Roaring Fork, some two miles from the intrenchments of the enemy; the bridge had been destroyed, and the remainder of the day was spent in rebuilding the bridge, and in some general preliminary reconnaissances. On the morning of the 10th, the 9th Ohio and Loomis's Battery were sent out as an escort to Lieutenant Poe, of the Topographical Engineers, charged with the reconnaissance of the enemy's position. His pickets were handsomely driven in, and the reconnaissance pushed to within two hundred yards of his works, with a loss of but one man killed and one wounded, on our part. The nature of the ground, and the dense thickets surrounding the enemy's works, rendered Lieutenant Poe's task one of extreme difficulty. The general result, confirmed by my own personal observations, was, that the enemy's position was well selected, near the foot of the mountain, where the road enters the pass. Its very considerable natural strength had been increased by rough intrenchments, and by a quantity of timber felled on all the front and flank approaches, which presented great obstacles to an attack. It was clear that a direct attack could succeed only after a great sacrifice of life, and the result of such an undertaking by perfectly raw troops was at least doubtful; I therefore determined to attempt to turn the position by our right, in conformity with the intention expressed in a letter of July 5, to the General-in-chief, in which I stated that I expected to find the enemy in position on Rich Mountain, just west of Beverly; that I should, if possible, turn the position to the south, and thus occupy the Beverly road in his rear; to repeat the maneuver of Cerro Gordo. I added, that I would not depart from my intention of gaining success by maneuvering rather than by fighting, as I was not willing to throw my raw troops into the teeth of artillery and intrenchments, if it were possible to avoid it. The 13th, 14th, and 15th Indiana had now arrived, or were within a day's march.

    I committed the charge of the turning movement

to General Rosecrans, with a command consisting of the 8th, 10th, and 13th Indiana, the 19th Ohio, and Burdsall's Ohio cavalry; the effective force of the infantry was eighteen hundred and forty-two. As the route to be pursued by General Rosecrans was in few places more than a mountain path, while at others a new road had to be cut as they advanced, it was impossible to move artillery with this column. His instructions, which were given on the evening of the 10th, were, that he should move at 4 A.M. on the 11th, and follow a path which led up a ravine to the summit of Rich Mountain, about a mile south of the point where the turnpike from Buckhannon to Beverly crosses the crest at Hart's farm. He was provided with a guide. Upon gaining the crest, he was to attack any force that might be there, and gain possession of the turnpike; then, taking proper precautions to guard his rear in the direction of Beverly, he was to move immediately to the west upon the rear of Pegram's defences. He was also instructed to send back a messenger every hour to report his progress. I also informed him that a little before noon I would have the rest of the troops in position to attack Pegram's works in front, the moment I heard the sound of his musketry immediately in the rear.

In accordance with these instructions, General Rosecrans moved on the route indicated, and, after an exceedingly difficult and toilsome march, gained the crest of Rich Mountain unopposed, at about one o'clock. He rapidly formed his command, and advanced along the crest towards the turnpike, before reaching which he encountered the enemy's skirmishers, who were soon driven in upon their supports at Hart's farm. This fore numbered some six hundred men, and had two guns; a small and hastily constructed log shelter was their only intrenchment. General Rosecrans soon attacked this force in the most gallant manner, and after a very spirited contest, drove them in confusion, and captured their two guns. The fugitives retired to Pegram's intrenchments. His men being fatigued, General Rosecrans now halted at 2 P.M., in the position he had won, and failed to carry out his orders to move on the rear of Pegram's works. At the hour agreed upon, a little before noon, I formed the regiments remaining with me (the 3d, 4th, and 9th Ohio, 14th and 15 Indiana, Howe's and Loomis's Batteries) in position to attack in front.

I received no message from General Rosecrans after a dispatch dated 11 A.M. Remaining in person immediately in rear of the picket line, I anxiously awaited news from Rosecrans, or the sound of his approaching musketry. We heard the firing at Hart's farm, but it was distant and stationary, and there was no indication of Rosecrans's approach. Soon after the cessation of the distant firing, an officer was observed to ride into the intrenchments and address the garrison; we could not distinguish the words he uttered, but his speech was followed by prolonged cheering, which impressed many with the belief that it had fared badly with our detachment.

While waiting, I again sent Lieutenant Poe to find a position from which our artillery could command the works. Late in the afternoon, I received his report that he had found one, and immediately sent a working party to cut a road to it. It was too late to get the guns in position before dark, and, as I had not yet received a word from General Rosecrans, I returned to camp with the command, leaving only the pickets, and a guard for the working party. Being now somewhat alarmed as to the fate of our detachment, I determined to put the guns in position immediately after day break, and, after shelling the works, to attack, in order to relieve Rosecrans.

As the troops were much fatigued, some delay occurred in moving from camp in the morning; and just as the guns were moving into position, the pickets sent intelligence that the enemy had evacuated their works during the night, and fled over the mountains, leaving their wounded, all their guns, means of transportation, ammunition, tents, and baggage. Then, for the first time since 11 o'clock the preceding day, I heard from General Rosecrans, who now informed me of what had transpired. Leaving Rosecrans's command to rest, and take care of the captured property, I pushed on without a moment's delay to Beverly, with the rest of the command. On reaching that place, I at once posted a portion of the troops in position to resist Garnett, should he endeavor to reach Huttonsville; and another portion to repel any reinforcements to the enemy arriving from the direction of the latter place.

When Colonel Pegram abandoned his works, he endeavored to join General Garnett at Laurel Hill; but the position of our troops preventing this, he was reduced to the alternative of starvation or surrender. On the morning of the 13th, he sent to me a messenger with a proposition to surrender, and I at once received his command as prisoners. A portion of his command had escaped singly through the mountains, but the number included in the surrender was 33 officers and 560 men. Had General Rosecrans been able to follow his instructions and moved direct upon Pegram, none of his command could have escaped. At 1 P.M. on the 12th, immediately after reaching Beverly, instructions were sent to General Rosecrans to forward the wounded to that place, and, leaving a small guard over the severely wounded and the captured property, to move his command at once to Beverly. Receiving definite information, during the night of the 12th and 13th, that General Garnett had retreated to the Leedsville and St. George road, and that the turnpike from Beverly to Philippi was clear, I at once, as will hereafter appear, gave the necessary orders for the pursuit of Garnett, and, on the morning of the 13th, marched to Huttonsville with the 3d, 4th, and 9th Ohio, and the 14th and 15th Indiana. Information had reached me that Colonel Scott's Virginia regiment, which had reached Beverly too late to support Pegram, had returned to Huttonsville; and captured official letters showed that strong reinforcements were on the march from Staunton; I therefore determined to lose no time in the endeavor to gain the Cheat Mountain Pass. We reached Huttonsville on the afternoon of the 13th, driving out a small cavalry force, and occupied the debouche of the pass. On the next day, with a strong advanced guard, well supported, I went to the summit of Cheat Mountain, and descended to the river on the other side. No enemy was encountered, although the pass presented many very strong positions, and the evidences of hasty flight were frequently met with, in the shape of abandoned baggage and camp-equipage. Making arrangements for intrenching and holding the pass, I left the 3d Ohio, 14th and 15th Indiana, Loomis's battery, and Burdsall's cavalry, under Brigadier-General Schleich, to hold the position, and on the 16th returned to the more central position of Beverly with the 4th and 9th Ohio, Howe's Battery, and Barker's Illinois cavalry company.

It is now time to revert to the measures taken for the pursuit of the forces under General Garnett. That officer, during the night of the 11th and 12th, upon hearing the result of the affair of Rich Mountain, immediately took steps to effect his retreat. During the night he abandoned his position at Laurel Hill, and marched towards Beverly. Arriving within five miles of that place, he found that it was impossible to escape in that direction, and at once retraced his steps to Leedsville, obstructing the roads behind him by felling trees.

Unfortunately, the extreme darkness of the night prevented the discovery of the evacuation by General Morris's pickets, until shortly after daylight. The usual difficulty and delay in getting new troops started on the march, and the necessity of feeling the way cautiously through so difficult a country, gave the enemy still further advantage, so that it was late in the afternoon before our advance reached Leedsville; the main body of the command did not get up until late at night, notwithstanding all the efforts of General Morris. At 4 A.M. on the 13th, General Morris resumed the pursuit, over very difficult mountain roads, in a heavy rain.

His advance, consisting of the 14th Ohio, 7th and

9th Indiana, and a section of Barnett's Battery, overtook the enemy towards midday at the main fork of Cheat River. Under the direction of Captain Benham, of the United States Engineers, the enemy was promptly attacked, and driven in disorder; the greater part of his baggage, and all his guns, were captured or soon abandoned, and General Garnett himself, while gallantly striving to rally his rear-guard, was killed. So prompt had been the conduct of the advance guard, that the action was over just as General Morris came up with the main body. The result of this brilliant affair at Carrick's Ford was a loss to the enemy of some twenty killed, fifty prisoners, and two colors, besides their train and guns. General Morris's command, which for thirty-six hours had been almost without food, and had made a most difficult march, was now too much fatigued to render further pursuit possible.

During the evening of the 12th I informed General Hill, then at Grafton, that General Garnett had abandoned Laurel Hill the previous night, and was then moving towards Eastern Virginia *via* Leedsville and St. George, and directed him to take the field at once, with all the force he could make available, to cut off the enemy's retreat. He was also informed that directions had been sent to Colonel Charles J. Biddle, commanding two regiments of Pennsylvania State troops at Cumberland, to move at once to Rowlesburg by express trains, and report to General Hill for duty. The latter was also instructed to withdraw several companies of the Railroad guards towards Wheeling and Parkersburg, and concentrate them by special trains at Rowlesburg or Oaklands, and that no time was to be lost. He was also informed that all the guns and baggage at Rich Mountain had been captured, and that, at the time of writing, the evening of the 12th, Garnett was some six miles from Leedsville on the St. George Road, with Morris in pursuit. General Hill acknowledged the receipt of this letter, and stated that measures were taken to obey the orders.

A railway bridge having been destroyed by the enemy west of Cumberland, it was impossible for Colonel Biddle to carry out his orders without cars sent to him from the west; this could not be accomplished in time, and Colonel Biddle was obliged to remain near New Creek, where he rendered all the service in his power, and displayed during the next few days, as he had already done in the past, great activity and intelligence.

On the 13th, General Hill started with some two thousand five hundred men, followed by considerable supports, which were rapidly arriving by rail, and, on the morning of the 14th, arrived at a point beyond the Red House, one and a half miles from the remnants of Garnett's army, who, starved, exhausted, and disorganized, were seeking a little rest before continuing their rapid retreat. For some reason which I have never yet understood, and which the pressure of more important cares soon prevented me from following up, he here abandoned the pursuit, and ordered a retrograde movement when the game was apparently in his grasp. On the night of the 15th he again resumed the pursuit; on learning which, I at once telegraphed to him that, in my opinion, he should have attacked the enemy on the morning of the 14th, and that he had then permitted the favorable moment to pass; that I could see no good result likely to follow from his then too extended movement, which was not in the spirit of his instructions, which were to cut off the enemy's retreat, and not to go into the heart of Virginia; that if he was not directly on the enemy's track, and sure to cut him off, he would, on the receipt of the dispatch, abandon the pursuit, which he did.

The result of these operations was thus to give us undisputed control of all that portion of Western Virginia north of the Great Kanawha, and of the passes leading in from the east. The enemy lost their general killed, and his second in command taken prisoner; all their guns, transportation, baggage, camp equipage, etc.; about one thousand in killed and prisoners, several colors, and many small arms; the remains of their force were entirely disorganized. Our own losses in all these affairs were a little less than one hundred men killed and wounded. From the best information that could be obtained, the total effective force in the district under the command of General Garnett was about eight thousand men.

While these events were in progress, our affairs in the Kanawha Valley became somewhat threatening. On the 16th of July General Cox was at the mouth of the Pocataligo, with four companies of the 11th Ohio, the whole of the 12th and 21st Ohio, five companies of the 1st Kentucky, four guns, and an imperfectly equipped company of raw cavalry. The remaining five companies of the 1st Kentucky were at Ripley, under orders to advance to Sissonville; three companies of the 11th were at Point Pleasant, guarding the depot; the

2nd Kentucky was on the march from Guyandotte *via* Barboursville, where, on the 16th, they defeated and drove out a force of six hundred of the enemy. General Cox labored under great disadvantages; his cavalry amounted to little or nothing; his artillery was weak and insufficiently manned; his land transportation entirely inadequate, and his supplies deficient. He moved close to the river, carrying his baggage on steamers. He marched an advanced guard on each bank, and held a regiment on steamers, ready to land on either shore, as might be necessary. Late on the 16th he was joined by the 2nd Kentucky; his force then being about three thousand four hundred men.

The difficulties in the way of his advance were such, that on the 17th he recommended that a part of the force under my immediate command should move into the upper part of the Kanawha Valley from the north; this request was repeated on the 19th. On that day, Colonel Lowe, of the 12th Ohio, with his own regiment, a detachment from the 21st Ohio, a few cavalry, and two guns, in all ten hundred and twenty men, came in contact with the enemy on the banks of Scary Creek. Colonel Lowe at once attacked, and, according to his report, was on the point of achieving success, when his ammunition gave out, and reinforcements arrived to the enemy; when he fell back in good order, with a loss of nine killed, thirty-eight wounded, and nine missing. He estimated the enemy's original force at sixteen hundred, their reinforcements at six hundred. On the second day after this affair the enemy fell back on Charleston.

Upon receiving information of these events, I determined to move at once in person to the Kanawha

Valley via Suttonsville, Summersville, and Dogwood Ridge, and thus cut off whatever force might be in the lower valley. The troops designated to accompany me were the 4th, 6th, 7th, 9th, and 13th Ohio, and 1st Virginia. The preparations were being rapidly made, the troops were in motion to the rendezvous, and General Cox had been informed of my general plans, when, on the 22d July, I received the order directing me to turn over my command to General Rosecrans, and proceed at once to Washington, to assume command of the troops in that vicinity.

At the time of taking the field in the Department of the Ohio, the following was the composition of the staff:

Major Seth Williams, Assistant Adjutant-General; Captain N.H. McLean, Assistant Adjutant-General; Major R.B. Marcy, Acting Inspector-General; Captain John H. Dickerson, Chief Quartermaster; Captain R. Saxton, Assistant Quartermaster; Captain William Craig, Assistant Quartermaster; Captain W.W. Burns, Chief Commissary; Captain R. Macfeely, Assistant Commissary; Surgeon J.J.B. Wright, Medical Director; Surgeon G.G. Shumard, Surgeon-General, Ohio State Troops; Captain H.W. Benham, Senior Engineer; Lieutenant O.M. Poe, Topographical Engineer; Captain C.P. Kingsbury, Chief of Ordnance; Lieutenant S. Crispin, Assistant Chief of Ordnance; Colonel T.M. Key, Judge Advocate; Lieutenant L.A. Williams, A.D.C.; Lieutenant Jos. Kirkland, A.D.C.; Colonel F.W. Lander, Volunteer Aid-de-Camp; Colonel William M. Dunn, Volunteer Aid-de-Camp.

It was through the cordial support and earnest efforts of these officers that it became possible to organize the troops and achieve success in the field. Colonel Lander accompanied, by my order, the troops who moved in May from Parkersburg to Grafton, and also the columns to Philippi, where he took a prominent part in the affair. Subsequently, at Rich Mountain, he accompanied the column under General Rosecrans, and there, too, distinguished himself in the encouragement and example he afforded the troops by his cool bravery under a severe fire.

In this brief campaign the telegraph was extensively used in the field of operations; the line was constructed as the army marched forward, and we were seldom without an office at head-quarters. Great credit is due to the superintendent, Mr. A. Stager, for his energy and intelligence.

I cannot close this brief narrative without bearing testimony to the good conduct, enthusiasm, and endurance of the young troops whom I then commanded. That they would be courageous was to be expected; but the patience and endurance they evinced under long marches, privations, and fatigue, exceeded all my anticipations. Their demeanor in this, their first campaign, gave promise of the achievements in which they have since participated on many hard-fought fields.

SELECTED CORRESPONDENCE

On the following pages are a selection of written letters and military telegraphs—some transcribed and some actual scans of existing documents—from the time period of McClellan's text. They are arranged in chronological order.

These documents are courtesy the collection of the United States Library of Congress.

TELEGRAPH
*From George B. McClellan to Winfield Scott,
June 26, 1861*

June 26 1861

Grafton Va

A letter of Genl Buckner to Gov Magoffin dated Louisville June tenth (10th) has just reached me through the newspapers It fills me with astonishment I can scarcely believe that he wrote It is an entire misconception & is incorrect throughout The arrangement & stipulations spoken of by him were got within my authority or my imagination The interview was purely personal solicited by him several times & granted by me mainly in the hope of reclaiming to the cause of the union an old & intimate friend my views of the political relations between the General Government & the state of Kentucky were radically different from these attributed to me in his letter. The whole interview was to me inconclusive & unsatisfactory & the only thing in the nature of a stipulation made between us was his voluntary proffer to attack & drive out any secession troops which might enter Kentucky May I ask that you will explain this fully to the President & cabinet I write more fully.

G. B. McClellan
Maj Genl

TELEGRAPH

From George B. McClellan to Edward D. Townsend, July 12, 1861

July 12 1861

Hd Qrs Dept of the Ohio
Rich Mountain Va.

Col E. D Townsend

We are in possession of all the enemy's works up to a point in sight of Beverly. Have taken all his guns a very large amount of wagons tents &c. Every thing he had a large number of prisoners many of whom wounded several officers prisoners they lost many killed we have lost in all perhaps twenty (20) killed and forty (40) wounded of whom all but two (2) or three (3) in the column under Gen Rosecrans which turned the position. Mass of enemy escaped through the woods entirely disorganized among prisoners Dr Taylor formerly of the army Col Pegram was in command Rosecrans column left Camp yesterday morning & marched some eight (8) miles through the mountains reaching turnpike some two (2) or three (3) miles in rear of the enemy. Defeated an advanced force taking a couple of Guns, I had position ready for twelve (12) Guns near main Camp and as

Guns were moving up ascertained that Enemy had retreated.

I am now pushing on to Beverly a part of Rosecrans' troops being now within three (3) miles of it Our success complete and almost bloodless Doubt whether Wise & Johnson will unite and overpower me——Behavior of troops in action and towards prisoners admirable.

G. B. McClellan
Maj Gen Comd'g

United States Military Telegraph.

Received July 13th 1861.

From Beverly Va 13

Col E D Townsend.

"Success of today is all that I could desire. We captured six (6) brass cannon of which one (1) rifled, all their camp equipage & transportation even to his caps. The number of tents will probably reach two hundred (200) and more than sixty (60) wagons their killed & wounded will amount to fully hundred & fifty (150) at least one hundred

(100) prisoners & more coming in constantly. I know already of ten (10) officers killed & prisoners, their retreat complete. Occupied Beverly by a rapid march, Garnett abandoned his camp early this morning, leaving much of his equipage. He came within a few miles of Beverly but our rapid march turned him back in great confusion and he is now retreating on the road to St George. I have ordered Gen Morris to follow him up closely. I have telegraphed for the two (2) Penna Regts at

United States Military Telegraph.

Received July 1861.

From (2)

Cumberland to join Genl Hill at Rowlesburg. The Genl is concentrating all his troops at Rowlesburg and cut off Garnett's retreat near West Union or if possible St George. I may say that we have driven out some ten thousand (10000) troops strongly entrenched with the loss of eleven (11).

10754

Killed & Thirty five (35) wounded. Previous returns found here show Garnett's force to have been ten thousand (10000) men. They were eastern Virginians, Georgians, Tennesseans and I think Carolinians. To-morrow I can give full details as to prisoners &c. Will move on Huttonsville tomorrow and endeavor to seize the Cheat mountain pass where there are now but few troops. I hope that Genl. Cox has by this time driven Wise out of the Kanawha Valley; in that case I shall

United States Military Telegraph.

Received July _____ 1861.

From _____

To _____

have accomplished the object of Liberating Western Virginia. I hope the General will approve my operations.

Geo. B. McClellan
Maj Genl Comdg
Dept of Ohio

2 P.M.

10755

Recd - July 13, 1861.
Beverly —

To Col. E. D. Townsend —

Have received from Pegram proposition for surrender with his officers and remnant of his command say Six hundred (600) men — Have accepted surrender agreeing to treat them with kindness due prisoners of War but stating that it was not in my power to relieve them from any liability incurred by taking arms against the United States — They are said to be extremely penitent & determined never again to take arms against the General Government. I shall have nearly Nine hundred (900) or One thousand prisoners to take care of when Pegram comes in — The question is an embarrassing one — Please give me immediate instructions by telegraph, as to disposition to be made of the officers & men taken prisoners of war — [apparently something omitted] I recommend that course as in many instances calculated to produce an excellent effect upon the deluded masses of the Rebels — The latest accounts make the loss of the Rebels in killed some one hundred & fifty "

Signed { G. B. McClellan
Major Genl
U.S.A.

United States Military Telegraph.

Received July 15th 1861.
From Huttonsville 14th.
To Col Townsend.

Garnett & forces routed! His Baggage &one (1) Gun taken! His army demoralized! Garnett killed! We have annihilated the enemy in Western Virginia & have lost thirteen (13) Killed and not more than forty (40) wounded. We have in all Killed at least two hundred (200) of the enemy & their prisoners will amount to at least one thousand (1.000) Have taken seven (7) Guns in all. I still look for the capture of the remnant of Garnett's army by Genl Hill. The troops defeated are the crack Regts of Eastern Virginia aided by Georgians Tennesseeans & Carolinians. Our success is complete and secession is killed in this country.

G B McClellan
Maj. Genl Comdg.

.03 m.

TELEGRAPH
From George B. McClellan to Abraham Lincoln,
July 17, 1861

July 17 1861.

Head Quarters
Beverly

I learn that the appointment of Gen J J Reynolds of Indiana as Brig Genl of three (3) years troops was determined upon some time since I respectfully ask your excellency that he may receive his Commission at once I need his services without delay he should be the first appointment from his state the Gov't has lost much and I have suffered much for the want of Capable General Officers Do give me Reynolds and if Convenient notify him and myself by telegraph

G. B McClellan
Maj Genl

TELEGRAPH

*From Winfield Scott to George B. McClellan,
July 18, 1861*

U. S. Army, Beverly, Va

Head Quarters of Army July 18. 1861

Your suggestions in respect to Staunton would be admirable, like your other conceptions and acts—with support. McDowell, yesterday, drove the enemy beyond Fairfax C. H.—He will attack the entrenched camp at the Manassas Junction, to day. Beaten there, the enemy may retreat both upon Richmond and the Shanandoah Valley, where Patterson is doing nothing. He will lose 18 regiments, by discharges, in about a week. I may re-inforce him, in that time, sufficiently, to enable you with him, to bag Johnston in that valley, if the latter has not been permitted to send his principal force to Beauregard. If you come to Staunton, and McDowells victory, at the Junction, be complete, he may, with Patterson, give you a hand about Winchester. I will telegraph you again to day

(signed) Winfield Scott

Recd. July 20, 1861 —

From Beverly 19th July —

To Col. E. D. Townsend —

Cox checked on the Kanawha. He fought something between a victory & a defeat. A wounded Col. of ours taken prisoner and a possibility of having lost two Colonels and a Lieut Col. who amused themselves by a Reconnaissance beyond the picketts — Have ordered him to remain where he is and will start as soon as possible to cut Wise's lear and relieve our Credit — In heavens name give me some General Officers who understand their profession. I give orders & find some who cannot execute them unless I stand by them —

Unless I command every column I cannot be sure of success. Give me such men as Marcy — Stevenson — Seckett — Lander Etc. and I will answer for it with my life that I meet with no disasters — Had my orders been executed from beginning, our success would have been brief & final —

Signed G. B. McClellan
Major Genl

Courtesy the collection of Tim McKinney

AFTERWORD
Tim McKinney

Born in Philadelphia on December 3, 1826, George Brinton McClellan was a man of keen intellect whose rendezvous with destiny would bring him to the edge of greatness—and would indelibly place his name in the annals of American history.

After graduating second in his class from West Point in 1846, he was assigned to the elite engineer corps. During the Mexican War he served with distinction as a lieutenant on the staff of General Winfield Scott. In 1848 McClellan returned to West Point where he taught engineering until 1851. Over the next six years, he worked on a variety of important Army engineering projects. Most notable among these was his survey from 1853 to 1854 for a Northern Pacific Railroad route across the Cascade Range. On January 16, 1857, he resigned his Army commission to become Chief Engineer of the Illinois Central Railroad. In this capacity, his organizational skills earned the respect of the railroad's attorney, Abraham Lincoln. In 1860, McClellan became president of the Ohio and Mississippi Railroad, a subsidiary of the Illinois Central.

With the outbreak of the Civil War in 1861, he returned to the Army as commander of the Department of Ohio. Initially appointed by Ohio's Governor William Dennison, he was soon placed by President Lincoln as second in command to Gen. Winfield Scott. His assignments included: major general, Ohio volunteers,

April 1861; commander of Ohio Militia, April 23–May 13, 1861; major general, United States Army, May 14, 1861; commanding Army of Occupation, West Virginia, Department of the Ohio, May 13–July 23, 1861; commanding Military Division of the Potomac, July 25–August 15, 1861; commanding Army and Department of the Potomac, August 15, 1861–November 9, 1862; and commander-in-chief, United States Army, November 5, 1861, until March 11, 1862.

During June and July 1861, General McClellan helped clear western Virginia (present West Virginia) of organized Confederate resistance. His successes in the mountains of West Virginia propelled him to national prominence, and on July 16, 1861, he received the formal thanks of the United States Congress. After the Union defeat at the battle of Manassas on July 21, 1861 Gen. McClellan was called to Washington and given command of the Department of the Potomac. His engineering and organizational skills were immensely valuable in creating the mighty Army of the Potomac.

In November, 1861, President Lincoln appointed the 35-year old general to succeed Winfield Scott as General-in-Chief of the Union Armies. Reflecting public opinion, the Lincoln administration pressed for an early offensive but McClellan insisted on adequate training for his troops and equipment for his army. His tendency toward overcaution very quickly began to undermine the confidence held in him by the public and the president.

In March of 1862 he was relieved of his supreme command but retained command of his Army of the Potomac. In April, McClellan advanced on Richmond by way of the Peninsula between the James and York

Rivers. Although his plan was a good one and its initial movements promising, he very rapidly allowed his army to get bogged down and he began siege operations at Yorktown. This delay allowed the Southern commanders to bring in reinforcements. Though his army survived a Confederate counterattack at the Battle of Seven Pines, his luck would not hold.

In June, General Lee attacked him in the battles known as the Seven Days. Here McClellan failed to take the opportunity to strike at Richmond along the poorly defended south side of the Chickahominy River. Rather than taking the offensive with his superior forces, he ordered a dangerous change of base from the York to the James River. A number of bloody battles ensued as a result of these movements, and although McClellan's forces were victorious in these fights, the overall campaign was a dismal failure. Stung by intense criticism of his command and realizing the opportunity to take Richmond had passed, McClellan entrenched at Harrison's Landing and began blaming everybody from the president to the War Department for his failure. Subsequently the decision was made in Washington to transfer most of McClellan's men to General John Pope's army in northern Virginia. McClellan became a favorite target of the northern press who denounced him as "Mac the Unready."

In the summer of 1862, General Pope's army was defeated at the Battle of Second Manassas. With his men streaming back into the Washington fortifications, the Lincoln Administration turned once again to General McClellan, who began immediately to refit and reorganize his massive army. McClellan did not have long to accomplish his work as Lee's Confederates invaded Maryland in early September. Advancing to confront Lee, he moved uncharacteristically fast when some of his men found a copy of General Lee's orders for the movement of his troops.

General Lee fought several delaying actions along South Mountain to gain sufficient time to reconcentrate his divided army. During this time General McClellan's infamous caution returned. He allowed his mighty army to slow down, thus giving Lee the opportunity to concentrate the majority of his command at Antietam, Maryland.

With a major battle on the horizon, it seemed that providence had granted McClellan an opportunity for a decisive victory. His army heavily outnumbered that of his enemy, whose back was against the Potomac River. McClellan, however, was not up to the task. He attacked piecemeal and his attacks failed to destroy Lee's command. Following a horrendous battle known as the bloodiest day of the Civil War, Lee's army escaped back into Virginia. President Lincoln was deeply disappointed with Lee's escape, but nevertheless used the "victory" to issue his Emancipation Proclmation.

In the face of mounting criticism over his failure to win a decisive victory at Antietam, General McClellan began anew calling for more men and additional equipment. His perceived dilatory tactics caused the Lincoln administration to lose patience with the "Hero of Rich Mountain," and on November 9, 1862, McClellan was officially relieved of command by the War Department. Returning to his home at Trenton, New Jersey, he became active in politics and in 1864 challenged Lincoln as the Democratic nominee for president. McClellan's candidacy was at first a matter of serious concern for the White House, as it appeared the former general might actually defeat Lincoln. Union victories diminished the public's war weariness, however, and McClellan won just three states.

Embarrassed by his poor showing, General McClellan resigned from the army on election day. Afterward he traveled extensively with his family in Europe and was later chief engineer of the New York City department of docks. He also served as Governor of New Jersey from 1878-1881. He wrote *McClellan's Own Story*, published in 1887, in defense of his military record.

George Brinton McClellan died unexpectedly of heart failure at Orange, New Jersey on October 29, 1885. The following day the *New York Times* announced his death to the nation: "The sudden death of the soldier who organized the Army of the Potomac and commanded it through the first stages of its career will occasion widespread sorrow among thousands of his old comrades and, indeed, throughout the country. The traits which caused him to be loved and respected by so many of those who served under him will be freely recalled, and not the least cordial of the tributes to his courtesy, his kindliness, and his integrity will come from those who in bygone years were arrayed against him either in the arena of politics or in the deadly strife of battle. Indeed, the bitter controversy over the value of the military services of Gen. McClellan rendered to the country, long ago subsided. . . . Between detraction on the one hand and adulation on the other, his place in history doubtless has already been found."

When Gen. McClellan wrote his *Report on the Organization and Campaigns of the Army of the Potomac in 1863*, a component of that report was his account of the West Virginia campaign reprinted here. At the time this report was written he had already been dismissed from active duty and had found himself and his campaigns the subject of considerable controversy. McClellan, of course, realized that his official reports were his best hope of setting the record straight as he saw it.

Given the perspective of more than a century, it is obvious his reports did little to assuage his critics, then or now. That fact is unfortunate, because his reports reflect the fact that in many cases the general possessed a better understanding of the facts and issues at hand than did his many detractors. With the war still raging and the possibility of Confederate victory alive, McClellan penned his reports without benefit of hindsight. Despite that fact, this report holds up well under modern scrutiny. It would not be so had he not fully understood the many complex challenges of the early campaigns.

McClellan notes early in his report that in the spring of 1861 it was difficult for people to believe a Civil War was actually at hand. Those familiar with the massive amounts of equipage and material manufactured and used during the war will marvel at McClellan's description of the weapons available at the onset of conflict. It is also interesting to note that Gen. McClellan did not consider slavery to be the cause of the war. Whether or not slavery was the genesis of the conflict, and if so to what extent, is a debate that lives even today.

He writes in this report that very early in the conflict he resisted numerous calls for the immediate occupation of West Virginia. Intense pressure was placed upon him to do so rapidly, but his reasoning for delaying immediate occupation is sound. Although the situation in West Virginia was quite complex with the populace divided in its sentiments, he writes that he considered the situation in Kentucky to be the most bitter.

McClellan's intellect and talents were heavily taxed in the early days of the war as he attempted to balance military and political priorities. That is a tough task in any war and was especially so in this one. When Governor Letcher of Virginia called out the state militia in early May 1861, it was believed by many that Ohio was soon to be invaded. The near panic and resulting outcry did not sway McClellan, however, as he accurately judged the Confederate actions to be strictly defensive. He also notes quite accurately in this report that very early in the conflict General Lee did not believe "any citizen" of Virginia would betray its interest. That fact contributed to the end result and was perhaps the first nail in the Confederate coffin in West Virginia.

On May 23, 1861, the secession ordinance was voted down in West Virginia and the statehood movement gaining speed. When, on May 26, Gen. McClellan received word that Confederate forces were moving on Wheeling and Parkersburg to destroy the railroad, the door was opened for his offensive operations. On that very day he issued orders for his men to cross the Ohio River and occupy the "Virginia Frontier." Hoping to diffuse the alarm that this movement would naturally cause in West Virginia, he issued a proclamation to the "Union Men of Western Virginia" in which he promised that all their rights would be "religiously respected."

Gen. McClellan was two years removed from the West Virginia campaign when this report was written. He had been stung by criticism that he was too cautious for prompt action. In this report he points out on two occasions that—when he ordered troops across the Ohio River—he did so on his own initiative. He writes that although he kept President Lincoln advised of developments, he received no "direct orders" to enter Virginia. He also states that he did not bring all of his available forces to bear in West Virginia because the "aspect of affairs in Missouri and Tennessee" was such that he did not feel at liberty to do so.

On June 20, 1861, Gen. McClellan determined that it was time for him to personally "take the field." He arrived at Parkersburg the following day in what he thought would be a "mere interlude" after which he would return to Cincinnati to resume preparations for the "more important movements upon East Tennessee." At Grafton, on June 23, McClellan issued another proclamation, this one addressed to "The Inhabitants of Western Virginia." Once again he sought to reassure the populace that their rights would be respected. He also stated that to his "great regret" he had found bushwhacking and Confederate guerilla activity to be rampant in the region. Two days later he issued a proclamation to his soldiers in which he pleaded with them to respect rights of person and property. This was a common theme with McClellan and no doubt he was sincere in that desire. War by its very nature however does not lend itself to "respect" and in a very short time it was seen that theory and reality would not meet in the mountains of West Virginia.

McClellan writes in this report that from the

very outset his efforts were hampered by the lack of experienced officers. Further, he observes that topography proved to be more of an obstacle to military operations than had been supposed. These are legitimate issues and were not an attempt on his part to cast blame elsewhere. Of the fighting at Rich Mountain, which of course was the victory that thrust McClellan into national prominence, he states that he commanded "perfectly raw troops." All of these factors—inexperienced officers and men, topography, and an inexperienced quartermaster department—had to be overcome.

Of the brief battle at Scary Creek, Putnam County, [W.] Va., on July 17, 1861, he states that Colonel Lowe's ammunition "gave out" and he was forced to retire from the field. As it happened, Union and Confederate forces both abandoned the field. When the Confederates realized the situation, they returned to claim a victory. Within a few days of that fight, Federal forces were defeated in the great battle of First Manassas. With that defeat, the "Hero of Rich Mountain" was called east to assume command of Union troops operating in the vicinity of Washington, D.C.

TIM MCKINNEY
Author, *The Civil War in Greenbrier County, West Virginia*; *Robert E. Lee at Sewell Mountain*; *The Civil War in Fayette County, West Virginia*; and *Robert E. Lee & the 35th Star*

INDEX

1st Kentucky Regiment 32, 42
1st Virginia Volunteers 14, 19, 27, 44
2d Kentucky Regiment 32, 43
2d Virginia Infantry 28
3d Ohio Regiment 28, 36, 38, 39
4th Ohio Regiment 28, 33, 36, 38, 39, 44
4th United States Artillery 28
6th Indiana Regiment 19, 27
6th Ohio Regiment 27, 44
7th Indiana Regiment 19, 27, 39
7th Ohio Regiment 28, 30, 44
8th Indiana Regiment 35
9th Indiana Regiment 19, 27, 40
9th Ohio Regiment 28, 30, 33, 36, 38, 39, 44
10th Indiana Regiment 28, 35
10th Ohio Regiment 28, 33
11th Ohio Regiment 32, 42
12th Ohio Regiment 32, 42, 43
13th Indiana Regiment 28, 34, 35
13th Ohio Regiment 44
14th Indiana Regiment 34, 36, 38, 39
14th Ohio Regiment 14, 19, 27, 39
15th Indiana Regiment 34, 36, 38, 39
15th Ohio Regiment 19, 27
16th Ohio Regiment 14, 19, 27
17th Ohio Regiment 28
18th Ohio Regiment 14, 27
19th Ohio Regiment 28, 35
20th Ohio Regiment 27
21st Ohio Regiment 32, 42, 43
22d Ohio Regiment 27
Baltimore & Ohio Railroad 12, 14, 28
Baltimore, Md. 3
Barboursville, [W.] Va. 32, 43
Barker, Captain 28
Barker's Cavalry 28, 39
Barnett, Colonel 27
Barnett's Battery 14, 19, 27, 40
Bellaire, Oh. 14
Benham, Captain H.W. 40, 44
Beverly, [W.] Va. 19, 20, 22, 29, 31, 33-35, 37-39
Biddle, Colonel Charles J. 40, 41
Branch Bank 30
Buckhannon, [W.] Va. 22, 27, 29-31, 33, 35
Burdsall, Captain 28
Burdsall's Cavalry 28, 35, 39
Burns, Captain W.W. 44
Cairo, Il. 7-9
Camp Dennison 9, 13
Cerro Gordo 34
Charleston, [W.] Va. 11, 32, 43
Charleston, S.C. 2
Cheat Mountain 38
Cheat Mountain Pass 20, 32, 38
Cheat River 20, 27, 28, 31, 40
Chicago Rifles 28
Chillicothe, Oh. 8
Cincinnati, Oh. 8, 9, 13, 17, 21, 23
Clarksburg, [W.] Va. 18, 22, 30, 31
Columbus, Ky. 7

Cox, General J.D. 32, 42-44
Craig, Captain William 44
Crispin, Lieutenant S. 44
Cumberland, Md. 40, 41
Dahn, Captain 28
Dahn's Virginia Battery 28
Davis, Garret 7
Dennison, Governor 3, 4, 10
Department of the Ohio 5, 9, 15, 17, 23, 25
Dickerson, Captain J.H. 20, 44
District of Kanawha 32
Dogwood Ridge 44
Dumont, Colonel 19
Dunn, Colonel William M. 44
Elk Bridge, [W.] Va. 30, 31
Elk Creek 30
Elliot's farm 32
Fairmont, [W.] Va. 14
Floyd, General 31
Fort Sumter 1
Gallipolis, Oh. 32
Garnett, General Robert S. 20, 21, 29, 30, 37-42
Gauley Bridge 32
Gauley River 28
Glenville, [W.] Va. 33
Grafton, [W.] Va. 11-14, 18, 19, 21, 23, 25, 27, 28, 40, 45
Great Kanawha River see Kanawha River
Great Kanawha Valley see Kanawha Valley
Guyandotte, [W.] Va. 32, 43
Harper's Ferry, [W.] Va. 12
Hart's farm 35, 36
Hill, Brigadier-General 27, 28, 31, 40, 41
Home Guards 7, 11
Howe, Captain 28
Howe's Battery 28, 36, 39
Huttonsville, [W.] Va. 22, 29, 30, 37, 38
Indiana Volunteers 19

Irwin, Colonel 14
Kanawha River, [Great] 8, 13, 28, 29, 42
Kanawha Valley, [Great] 12, 22, 31, 42-44
Kelly, Colonel B.F. 14, 18, 19
Key, Colonel T.M. 44
Kingsbury, Captain C.P. 44
Kirkland, Lieutenant Jos. 44
Lander, Colonel F.W. 44, 45
Laurel Hill, [W.] Va. 20, 22, 29, 31-33, 37, 39
Laurel Mountain 22
Lee, General Robert E. 11, 12
Leedsville, Va. 29, 30, 38-41
Letcher, Governor 11, 12
Lewisburg, [W.] Va. 29
Lincoln, Abraham 2, 18
Little Kanawha River 29
Little Miami Railroad 9
Loomis, Captain 28
Loomis's Battery 28, 30, 33, 36, 39
Louisville, Ky. 8
Lowe, Colonel 43
Lynchburg, Tn. 8
Macfeely, Captain R. 44
Marcy, Major R.B. 44
Marietta, Oh. 18
McCook, Colonel R.L. 33
McLean, Captain N.H. 44
Memphis, Tn. 7
Middle Fork Bridge 33
Mississippi River 9
Monongahela River 29
Moorefield, [W.] Va. 29
Morris, Brigadier-General T.A. 19, 20, 27, 28, 32, 33, 39-41
Morton, Governor 10
Nashville, Tn. 9
New Creek 41
Oaklands, [W.] Va. 40
Ohio Militia 27
Ohio River 16, 28

Ohio Volunteers 32
Parkersburg, [W.] Va. 11-14, 21, 31, 40, 45
Patterson, General 22, 23
Pegram, General 29, 30, 35-38
Pennsylvania State regiments 40
Philippi, [W.] Va. 18-20, 22, 27, 28, 30, 38, 45
Pocataligo River 42
Poe, Lieutenant O.M. 33, 34, 36, 44
Point Pleasant, [W.] Va. 32, 42
Porterfield, Colonel 11-13
Red House 41
Rich Mountain, [W.] Va. 20, 29, 34, 35, 39, 41, 45
Richmond, Va. 6, 8, 11, 12, 23
Ripley, [W.] Va. 32, 42
Roaring Fork 33
Romney, [W.] Va. 21
Rosecrans, Brigadier-General William S. 21, 28, 30, 33, 35-38, 44, 45
Rowlesburg, [W.] Va. 31, 40
Sandoval, Il. 8
Saxton, Captain R. 44
Scary Creek 43
Schleich, Brigadier-General 28, 30, 31, 33, 39
Scott, Colonel 38
Seymour, In. 8
Shumard, Surgeon G.G. 44
Sissonville, [W.] Va. 42, 44
St. George, [W.] Va. 29-31, 38, 40, 41
St. Louis arsenal 3
St. Louis, Mo. 7, 8
Stager, Mr. A. 45
Staunton, Va. 12, 29, 30, 38
Stedman, Colonel 14, 18
Summersville, [W.] Va. 44
Taylor County, [W.] Va. 11
Ten Mile Creek 32
Topographical Engineers 33

Tygart's Valley River 19, 29
Tyler, Colonel 30
Union City, Tn. 7
United States Engineers 40
Wabash River 8
Washington, D.C. 2, 4, 8, 18, 23, 44
Webster, [W.] Va. 19, 30
West Fork Monongahela River 29
West Union, [W.] Va. 29
Weston, [W.] Va. 30, 31
Wheeling, [W.] Va. 6, 12-14, 18, 19, 29, 40
Willey, Colonel 13
Williams, Lieutenant L.A. 44
Williams, Major Seth 44
Winchester, Va. 22, 23
Wise, General 31
Wood County, [W.] Va. 11
Wright, Surgeon J.J.B. 44
Yates, Governor 10